What Happens in Summer?

Sara L. Latta

Enslow Elementary

an imprint of

Enslow Publishers, Inc.

40 Industrial Road   PO Box 38
Box 398   Aldershot
Berkeley Heights, NJ 07922   Hants GU12 6BP
USA   UK

http://www.enslow.com

Words to Know

pollen (PAHL ehn)—
Tiny grains made
by flowers that
allow seeds to grow
into new plants.

Yellow pollen
is on this
flower and on
the bee's body.

tilt (TIHLT)—To tip
to one side. Earth
tilts as it goes
around the sun.

Earth is tilted.

Contents

What are the seasons?

Winter, spring, summer, fall—these are the four seasons of the year.

winter   spring

Each season lasts about three months. The seasons change from cold to warm, then back to cold. Summer is the warmest season.

summer   **fall**

When is it summer?

The earth goes around the sun one time each year. Earth **tilts** as it goes around the sun.

North Pole

Summer

Winter

When the North Pole tilts toward the sun, the north part of Earth has summer.

Earth's path around sun

Winter

Summer

South Pole

When the South Pole tilts toward the sun, the south part of Earth has summer.

The first day of summer in North America is around June 21.

How does Earth's tilt make summer weather warm?

Let's look at summer in the north part of Earth. The north part of Earth tilts toward the sun in summer. The sun's rays fall straight on this part of Earth. This makes summer sunlight very strong.

North Pole

North America

South America

South Pole

Here, the sun's rays hit Earth directly. Direct light is stronger than light at an angle. It is summer.

Here, the sun's rays hit Earth on an angle. These rays are not as strong. It is winter in the south part of Earth.

What else makes summer warm?

Summer days have more hours of sunlight than winter days. There is more time to warm the air, water, and land.

The summer heat also causes rain,
wind, lightning, and thunder.

How do summer days help plants grow?

Plants use sunlight to make food. Plants get water from summer rains. This food and water helps plants grow. From the short grass to tall trees, many plants grow fast in summer.

Many plants have colorful flowers in the summer. Bees and butterflies spread pollen from plant to plant. Then the plant can make seeds. The seeds will make new plants.

pollen

What do animals do in the summer?

Leafy trees and bushes make good homes for birds and other animals. There is plenty of food for the animals to eat. Young animals grow and learn about their world in the summer.

white-footed mouse

white-tailed deer

opossums

15

What do farmers do in the summer?

Summer is a busy time for farmers. The summer sunlight makes crops grow fast. Farmers grow wheat for our bread. They grow juicy peaches and crunchy carrots for us to eat.

What do children do in the summer?

Most schools have a summer break. This is a good time to go on a trip. Many people go swimming, hiking, or camping. What do you like to do on long summer days?

19

Do plants need sunlight to grow?

You will need:

- ❖ **potting soil**
- ❖ **4 small paper cups**
- ❖ **sunflower seeds or bean seeds**
- ❖ **water**
- ❖ **plastic wrap**

1. Put some potting soil into four small paper cups.

2. Press two or three seeds into the soil in each cup.

3. Pour some water into each cup.

4. Cover each cup with plastic wrap. Put the cups in a sunny spot. Check your pots every day. Don't let them dry out!

5. When the seeds start to sprout, remove the plastic wrap. Put two of the containers in a shady place. Leave the other two in the sunny spot. Which plants grow better? Why? As your plants grow, move them to a larger pot.

Learn More

Books

Branley, Franklyn, M. *Sunshine Makes the Seasons*. New York: HarperCollins Publishers, 2005.

Gerard, Valerie, J. *Summer: Signs of the Season Around North America*. Minneapolis: Picture Window Books, 2003.

Glaser, Linda. *It's Summer!* Brookfield, Conn.: Millbrook Press, 2003.

Stille, Darlene R. *Summer*. Minneapolis: Compass Point Books, 2001.

VanCleave, Janice. *Janice VanCleave's Science Around the Year*. New York: Wiley, 2000.

Web Sites

The National Center for Atmospheric Research and UCAR. "Kids' Crossing."
 <http://www.eo.ucar.edu/kids/index.html>

NASA KIDS. "The First Day of Summer."
 <http://kids.msfc.nasa.gov/news/2000/news%2Dsummer.asp>

The Weather Classroom.
 <http://www.weatherclassroom.com>

Index

Enslow Elementary, an imprint of Enslow Publishers, Inc.

Enslow Elementary® is a registered trademark of Enslow Publishers, Inc.

Copyright © 2006 by Enslow Publishers, Inc.

Library of Congress Cataloging-in-Publication Data

Latta, Sara L.
    What happens in summer? / Sara L. Latta.
       p. cm. — (I like the seasons!)
    Includes bibliographical references and index.
    ISBN 0-7660-2416-4 (hardcover)
    1. Summer—Juvenile literature.
    2. Seasons—Juvenile literature. I. Title. II. Series
    QB637.6.L38 2006
    508.2-dc22

                                        2005012444

Printed in the United States of America

10 9 8 7 6 5 4 3 2 1

Photo Credits: Antonia Reeve/Science Photo Library, p. 17; © Bill Beatty / Visuals Unlimited, p. 13; © Corel Corporation, pp. 4 (right), 5 (right), 22, 23; © David Cavagnaro / Visuals Unlimited, p. 12; © Dynamic Graphics, Inc., p. 18; © Gary Meszaros/Visuals Unlimited, p. 14; © Inga Spence/Visuals Unlimited, p. 16; © Jane McAlonan/Visuals Unlimited, p. 15 (top); © 2005 JupiterImages Corporation, pp. 4 (left), 5 (left), 8, 10, 19, 20; Mark Garlick/Science Photo Library, pp. 6–7; © Steve Maslowski/Visuals Unlimited, p. 15 (bottom); Stock Connection, p. 11; Tom LaBaff, p. 9.

Cover Photo: © agefotostock/SuperStock

Every effort has been made to locate all copyright holders of material used in this book. If any errors or omissions have occurred, corrections will be made in future editions of this book.

Series Literacy Consultant
Allan A. De Fina, Ph.D.
Past President of the New Jersey Reading Association
Professor, Department of Literacy Education
New Jersey City University

Science Consultant
Harold Brooks, Ph.D.
NOAA/National Severe Storms Laboratory
Norman, Oklahoma

Note to Parents and Teachers: The I Like the Seasons! series supports the National Science Education Standards for K–4 science. The Words to Know section introduces subject-specific vocabulary words, including pronunciation and definitions. Early readers may need help with these new words.